# BOOK OF PRAYERS

## *A COLLECTION OF DEAR AND SPECIAL PRAYERS*

*By*

## Jeannette Caballero

Prayers, as a solemn request for help, offer comfort.

We pray for guidance and protection.
We pray when life challenges test our limits.
We pray to praise God, and to give thanks.
Prayers are acts of faith and love, that have spiritual power to transform lives.
Prayers can be practiced spontaneously by anyone, anytime.

Father, into Thy hands I commend my Spirit.

Jesus Christ

# Table of Contents

# INTRODUCTION

This is a collection of special prayers, chosen for their mighty heritage, purpose or simple beauty. These prayers have been gathered with the intent to provide easy access to prayers for varied occasions. Some historical sacred prayers have been included. These prayers have given me comfort, hope, strength, thankfulness and a more loving spirit. I hope that it can do the same for others.

# ANIMA CHRISTI

Soul of Christ, sanctify me
Body of Christ, save me
Blood of Christ, refresh me
Water from Christ's side, wash me
Passion of Christ, strengthen me
O good Jesus, hear me
Within Thy wounds hide me
Suffer me not to be separated from Thee
From the malicious enemy, defend me
In the hour of my death call me
And bid me come unto Thee
That with thy saints I may praise Thee
Forever and ever
Amen

*Middle ages*

## THE LORD'S PRAYER

Our Father, who art in heaven,
hollowed be thy name.
Thy Kingdom come,
thy will be done,
on earth as it is in heaven
Give us this day our daily bread.
And forgive us our trespasses,
as we forgive those who trespass against us.
And lead us not into temptation,
but deliver us from evil.
For thine is the kingdom, the power and the glory, for ever and
ever.
Amen.


*Gospel of St. Matthew 6:9-13*

*The Angel of the Lord declared to Mary:*
*And she conceived of the Holy Spirit.*

## HAIL MARY

Hail Mary, full of grace,
the Lord is with thee;
blessed art thou among women
and blessed is the fruit of thy womb, Jesus.
Holy Mary, Mother of God,
pray for us sinners,
now and at the hour of our death.
Amen.

# PRAYER FOR TRUE WISDOM

Lord, Thou know better than I know myself
that I am growing older and will someday be old.
keep me from the fatal habit
of thinking I must say something
on every subject and on every occasion.

Release me from craving to straighten out
everybody's affairs.
Make me thoughtful, but not moody,
helpful but not bossy.
With my vast store of wisdom,
It seems as pity not to use it all,
but Thou know, Lord,
that I want a few friends left at the end.

Keep my mind free from the endless recital of details.
Give me wings to get to the point.
Seal my lips on my aches and pains.
They are increasing, and the love of the rehearsing them,
Is becoming ever sweeter.
As the years go by,
I dare not ask for grace enough to enjoy the tales of other's
pains,
but help me to endure them with patience.

I dare not ask for improved memory, only a growing humility,
and a lessening cocksureness,
when my memory seems to clash with that of others.
Teach me the glorious lesson that I could be occasionally
mistaken.

Keep me reasonably sweet, I do not want to be a saint,
some of them are so hard to live with,
but a sour old person is one of the crowning works of the devil.
Give me the ability to see good things in unexpected places,
and talents in unexpected people.
And grant me, O Lord,
the gift of having the grace to tell them so.
Amen.

*Nun's prayer from the 1700 century*

# THE BREASTPLATE OF ST. PATRICK - THE DEER'S CRY

I arise today through a mighty strength, the invocation of the Trinity,
through belief in the Threeness,
through confession of the Oneness of the Creator of creation.

I arise today through the strength of Christ with His Baptism,
through the strength of His Crucifixion with His Burial
through the strength of His Resurrection with His Ascension,
through the strength of His descent for the Judgement of Doom.

I arise today through the strength of the love of Cherubim
in obedience of Angels, in the service of the Archangels,
in hope of resurrection to meet with reward,
in prayers of Patriarchs, in predictions of Prophets,
in preachings of Apostles, in faiths of Confessors,
in innocence of Holy Virgins, in deeds of righteous men.

I arise today, through the strength of Heaven:
light of Sun, brilliance of Moon, splendor of Fire,
speed of Lightning, swiftness of Wind, depth of Sea,
stability of Earth, firmness of Rock.

I arise today, through God's strength to pilot me:
God's might to uphold me, God's wisdom to guide me,
God's eye to look before me, God's ear to hear me,
God's word to speak for me, God's hand to guard me,
God's way to lie before me, God's shield to protect me,
God's host to secure me:
against snares of devils, against temptations of vices,
against inclinations of nature, against everyone who
shall wish me ill, afar and near, alone and in a crowd.

I summon today all these powers between me (and these evils):
against every cruel and merciless power that may oppose my
body and my soul, against incantations of false prophets, against
black laws of heathenry,
against spells of women (any witch) and smiths and wizards,
against every knowledge that endangers man's body and soul.
Christ to protect me today
against poison, against burning, against drowning,
against wounding, so that there may come abundance of reward.

Christ  with me, Christ before me, Christ behind me, Christ in
me, Christ beneath me, Christ above me, Christ on my right,
Christ on my left, Christ in breadth, Christ in length,
Christ in height, Christ in the heart of every man who thinks of
me,
Christ in the mouth of every men who speaks of me,
Christ in every eye that sees me, Christ in every ear that hears
me.

I arise today through a mighty strength, the invocation of the Trinity,
through belief in the Threeness, through confession of the Oneness of the Creator of creation.
Salvation is of the Lord. Salvation is of the Lord.
Salvation is of Christ. May Thy Salvation, O Lord, be ever with us.

# CANTICLE OF BROTHER SUN AND SISTER MOON

Most High, all powerful, all good Lord,
All praise be Yours, all glory, all honor and all blessings.
To you alone, Most High, do we belong,
and no mortal lips are worthy to pronounce Your Name.

Praised be You my Lord with all Your creatures,
especially Sir Brother Sun,
who is the day through whom You give us light.
And he is beautiful and radiant with splendor,
of You Most High, he bears the likeness.

Praised be You, my Lord, through Sister Moon and stars,
in the heavens you have made them bright, precious and fair.

Praised be You, my Lord, through Brothers Wind and Air,
and fair and stormy, all weather's moods,
by which You cherish all that You have made.

Praised be You my Lord through Sister Water,
so useful, humble, precious and pure.

Praised be You my Lord through Brother Fire,
through whom You light the night and he is beautiful,
playful, robust and strong.

Praised be You my Lord through our Sister,
Mother Earth who sustains and govern us,
producing varied fruits and colored flowers and herbs.
Praised be You my Lord through those who grant pardon for
love of You
and bear sickness and trial.

Blessed are those who endure in peace,
By You Most High, they will be crowned.

Praised be You, my Lord through Sister Death,
from whom no one living can escape.
Woe to those who die in mortal sin!
Blessed are they She finds doing Your Will.

No second death can do them harm.
Praise and bless my Lord and give Him thanks,
and serve Him with great humility.
Amen.

*St. Francis of Assisi*

# PEACE PRAYER OF SAINT FRANCIS OF ASSISI

Lord, make me an instrument of your peace:
where there is hatred, let me sow love;
where there is injury, pardon;
where there is doubt, faith;
where there is despair, hope;
where there is darkness, light;
where there is sadness, joy.

O divine Master, grant that I may not so much seek
to be consoled as to console,
to be understood as to understand,
to be loved as to love.
For it is in giving that we receive,
it is in pardoning that we are pardoned,
and it is in dying that we are born to eternal life.
Amen

*Saint Francis of Assisi*

# A BLESSING FOR THE SICK OF SAINT FRANCIS OF ASSISI

Lord Jesus, when you were on earth, they brought the sick to you and you healed them all.
Today I ask you to bless all those in sickness, in weakness and in pain.

For those who are blind and who cannot see the light of the sun;
the beauty of the world, or the faces of their friends:
Bless your people, O Lord.

For those who are deaf and cannot hear the voices which speak to them:
Bless your people, O Lord.

For those who are helpless and who must lie in bed while others go out and in:
Bless your people, O Lord.

For those whose minds have lost their reason and those who are so nervous that they cannot cope with life:
Bless your people, O Lord.

For those who must face life under some handicap, those whose weakness means that they must always be careful:
Bless your people, O Lord.

For those suffering from debilitating or terminal illness and for

their caregivers:
Bless your people, O Lord.

For those who are near the hour of death and in their final struggle:
Bless your people, O Lord.

Father, your only Son took upon himself the sufferings and weaknesses of the whole human race, though his passion and cross he taught us how good can be brought out of suffering. Look upon our brothers and sisters who are ill, whom we now remember in a special way. In the midst of illness and pain, may they be united with Christ, who heals both body and soul. We ask this through Christ our Lord Amen.

Almighty God, as we ask your help for our brothers and sisters who are ill, we ask you to us to be healing people in our time and place. May your love touch others through us, and I help all people to live in peace.
We ask this through Christ our Lord Amen.

## MERCIFUL GOD, FILL OUR HEARTS

O merciful God, fill our hearts, we pray, with the graces of thy Holy Spirit, with love, joy peace, patience, gentleness, goodness, faithfulness, humility, and self-control.

Teach us to love those who hate us; to pray for those who despitefully use us; that we may be the children of thy love, our Father, who makes the sun to rise on the evil and the good and send rain on the just and the unjust.

In adversity grants us grace to be patient; in prosperity keep us humble; may we guard door of our lips; may we lightly esteem the pleasures of this world, and thirst for heavenly things; through Jesus Christ our Lord.

Amen.

*Anselm 1033-1109*

# TEACH MY HEART

O Lord my God,
teach my heart where and how to seek you,
where and how to find you.
Lord, if you are not here but absent,
Where shall I seek you?
But you are everywhere, so you must be here,
Why then do I not seek you?
Lord, I am not trying to make my way to your height,
For my understanding is in no way equal to that,
But I do desire to understand a little of your truth
Which my heart already believes and loves.
I do not seek to understand so that I may believe,
But I believe so that I may understand;
And what is more,
I believe that unless I do believe, I shall not understand.
Amen

*Anselm 1033-1109*

# THE UNIVERSAL PRAYER

We ask you, Master, to be our helper and protector.
Save those among us who are in distress;
have mercy on the humble; raise up the fallen;
show yourself to those in need; heal the sick;
turn back those of your people who wander; feed the hungry;
ransom our prisoners; raise up the weak; comfort the
discouraged.
Let all the nations know that you are the only God,
that Jesus Christ is your servant,
and that we are your people and the sheep of your pasture.

*Excerpt from St. Clement's letter to the church at Corinth.*

# SOUL CLENSING

O God, who has taught us Thy divine and saving oracles, enlighten the souls of us sinners for the comprehension of the things which have been before spoken, so that we may not only be seen to be hearers of spiritual things, but also doers of good deeds, striving after guileless faith, blameless life, and pure conversation.

Release, pardon, and forgive, O God, all our voluntary and involuntary sins, such as we committed in action and in word, knowingly and ignorantly, by night and by day, in mind and thought, forgive us all in goodness and love.

Sanctify, O Lord, our souls, bodies and spirits; examine our minds and search our consciences take from us all evil imaginations, all impurity of thought, all inclinations to lust, all depravity of conception, all envy, pride and hypocrisy, all falsehood, deceit and irregular living, all covetousness, vain glory and sloth; all malice, anger and wrath, all remembrance of injuries, all blasphemy and every motion of flesh and spirit that is contrary to the purity Thy Will.
Amen

*Liturgy of St. James.*

## WISDOM

Almighty God, give us wisdom to perceive you,
intellect to understand you,
diligence to seek you, patience to wait for you,
eyes to behold you,
a heart to meditate upon you, and life to proclaim you,
through the power of the Spirit of our Lord Jesus Christ.
Amen.

*Benedict of Nursia.*

# SUPPLICATION

Lo, fainter now lie spread the shades of night,
And upward spread the trembling gleams of morn,
Suppliant we bend before the Lord of Light,
And pray at early dawn,
That this sweet charity may all our sin
Forgive, and make our miseries to cease;
May grant us health, grant us the gift divine
Of everlasting peace.
Father Supreme, this grace on us confer;
And thou, O Son by an eternal birth:
With thee, coequal Spirit, comforter!
Whose glory fills the earth.
Amen.

*Pope Gregory I*

## PRAYER OF SAINT EPHREM

O Lord and Master of my life,
spare me from the spirit of apathy and meddling,
of idle chatter and love of power,
grant to me, your servant,
the spirit of integrity and humility,
of patience and love.
Yes, O Lord and God,
grant me the grace to be aware of my sins and not to judge
others,
for you are blessed, now and forever.
Amen

*Saint Ephrem*

# PRAYER TO YOUR GUARDIAN ANGEL

Angel of God, my guardian dear,
to whom God's love commits me here,
ever this day be at my side,
to light and guard, to rule and guide.
Amen.

*St. Anselm I Reginald of Canterbury.*

## A TRAVELERS PRAYER FOR SAINT CHRISTOPHER'S PROTECTION

Dear Saint Christopher, protect me today
in all my travels
along the road's way. Give your warning sign if danger is near
so that I may stop
while the path is clear.
Be at my window
and direct me through when the vision blurs from out the blue.
Carry me safely
to my destined place, like you carried Christ in your close
embrace. Amen.

*Author unknown*


## SAINT CHRISTOPHER'S PRAYER

Glorious Saint Christopher, you have inherited a beautiful
name,
Christ bearer, as a result of the wonderful legend
that while carrying people across a raging stream,
you also carried the Child Jesus Christ.
Teach us to be true Christ bearer to those who do not know
Him.
Protect all of us that travel both near and far,
and petition Jesus Christ to be with us always.
Amen.

## COME CREATOR SPIRIT- VENI CREATOR SPIRITUS

Come, Holy Spirit, Creator blessed,
keep our souls safe to rest;
come with Thy grace and heavenly aid
 and fill the hearts which Thou hast made.

To Thee Comforter, we cry,
to Thee, the Gift of God Most High,
The fountain of life, the Fire of love,
The soul's Anointing from above.

The sevenfold gifts of grace and Thine,
O Finger of the Hand Divine;
true promise of the Father Thou,
who does the tongue with speech endow.

Thy light to every thought impart
and shed Thy love in every heart;
the weakness of our mortal state,
with deathless might invigorate.

Drive far away our wily Foe,
and Thine abiding peace bestow;
If Thou be our protecting Guide,
no evil can our steps bring forth.

Make Thou to us the Father known;
teach us the eternal Son to own,
and Thee, whose name we ever bless,
of both the Spirit, to confess.

Praise we the Father and the Son
and Holy Spirit, with them One;
and may the Son on us bestow
the gifts that from the Spirit flow! Amen.

*Rabanus Maurus*

# PREPARING FOR STUDY, WRITING OR PRESENTATION

Master Creator,
who from the treasures of Your wisdom,
have established three hierarchies of angels,
have arrayed them in marvelous order
above the fiery heavens,
and have marshaled the regions
of the universe with artful skill.

You are proclaimed
the true font of light and wisdom,
and the primal origin
raised high beyond all.

Pour forth a ray of Your brightness
into the darkened places of my mind;
disperse from my soul the twofold darkness,
into which I was born:
sin and ignorance.

You make eloquent the tongues of infants.
Refine my speech
and pour forth upon my lips
the goodness of Your blessing.

Grant to me keenness of mind,
capacity to remember,
skill in learning,
subtlety to interpret,
and eloquence in speech.

May You guide
the beginning of my work,
direct its progress,
and bring it to completion.

You Who are true God and true Man,
Who live and reign, world without end.
Amen

*St. Thomas Aquinas*

# GOD'S VISION

O give me Samuel's heart,
a humble heart, that waits
where in Thy house Thou art.
Or watches at Thy gates;
By day and night, a heart that still
moves at the breathing of Thy will.

0 give me Samuel's mind,
a sweet, unmurmuring faith.
Obedient and resigned
to Thee in life and death,
that I may read with childlike eyes
Truths that are hidden from the wise.

*J D Burns*

## IRISH BLESSING

May the road rise to meet you,
May the wind be always at your back. May the sun shine warm
upon your face, The rains fall soft upon your fields.
And until we meet again,
May God hold you in the hollow of his hand. May God be with
you and bless you:
May you see your children's children. May you be poor in
misfortune,
Rich in blessings.
May you know nothing but happiness From this day forward.
May the road rise up to meet you
May the wind be always at your back
May the warm rays of sun fall upon your home And may the
hand of a friend always be near. May green be the grass you
walk on,
May blue be the skies above you,
May pure be the joys that surround you, May true be the hearts
that love you.

Ancient Celtic times. Attributed to Saint Patrick

## OLD IRISH BLESSING - MERRY WISHES

May love and laughter light your days, and warm your heart and home.

May good and faithful friends be yours, wherever you may roam.

May peace and plenty bless your world with joy that long endures.

May all life's passing seasons bring the best to you and yours.

# ARCHANGELS PRAYER

In the name of the Lord,
the God of Israel,
may Michael be at my right hand;
Gabriel at my left,
Uriel before me,
Raphael behind me,
and the dwelling of God be above my head.

*Medieval Jewish Prayer*

# SUB TUUM PRAESIDIUM - OLDEST KNOWN MARIAN PRAYER, TRACES BACK TO EGYPT

WE FLY TO THY PROTECTION - VATICAN TRANSLATION

We fly to Thy protection,
O Holy Mother of God.
Do not despise our petitions in our necessities,
but deliver us always from all dangers,
O Glorious and Blessed Virgin.


GOD BEARER - SHE, WHOSE OFFSPRING IS GOD

Under your mercy we take refuge,
Mother of God !
Our prayers, do not despise in necessities,
but from danger deliver us,
only pure, only blessed.

# VENI SANCTE SPIRITUS - GOLDEN MEDIEVAL SEQUENCE

Come, Holy Spirit,
and send out from heaven
the ray of your light.

Come, father of the poor,
come, giver of gifts, come light our hearts.

Greatest comforter,
sweet guest of the soul,
sweet consolation.

In labor, rest,
in temperateness, in tears solace.

O most blessed light,
fill the inmost heart of your faithful.

Without the nod of your head,
there is nothing in man,
nothing that is harmless.

Cleanse what is unclean,
parch what is parched,
heal what is wounded.

Bend that is inflexible,
warm what is chilled,
correct what has gone astray.

Give to your faithful,
who trust in you,
the sevenfold gift.

Give virtue's reward,
give salvation's end,
give joy eternal.

*Attributed to Pope Innocent Ill I Cardinal Stephen Langton.*

# SECOND PRAYER OF SAINT BASIL THE GREAT

We bless The, O most high God and Lord of mercy,
Who art ever doing numberless great and inscrutable things
with us,
glorious and wonderful; Who grant to us sleep for rest from our
infirmities,
and repose from the burdens of our much toiling flesh.
We thank Thee that Thou hast not destroyed us with our sins,
but hast loved us as ever, and though we are sunk in despair,
Thou has raised us up to glorify Thy power.
Therefore we implore Thy incomparable goodness,
enlighten the eyes of our understanding
and raise up our mind from the heavy sleep of indolence;
open our mouth and fill it with Thy praise,
that we may be able undistracted to sing and confess Thee,
Who art God glorified in all and by all, the eternal Father,
with Thy only-begotten Son,
and Thy all-holy and good and life-giving Spirit,
now and ever, and to the ages of ages.
Amen.

## HOLY SPIRIT

Breathe in me, O Holy Spirit,
that my thoughts may be holy.
Act in me, O Holy Spirit,
that my work, too, may be holy.
Draw my heart, O Holy Spirit,
that I may love only what is holy.
Strengthen me, O Holy Spirit,
that I may defend all that is holy.
Guard me, 0 Holy Spirit,
that I may always be holy.

*Saint Augustine*

# PARAGRAPH FROM CONFESSIONS

Almighty God, who knows our necessities before we ask,
and our ignorance in asking: set free thy servants from all
anxious thoughts for tomorrow;
give us contentment with thy good gifts;
and confirm our faith according as we see thy kingdom,
thou wilt not suffer us to lack of good thing;
through Jesus Christ our Lord.
Amen.

*Saint Augustine of Hippo*

# EVENING PRAYER OF SAINT AUGUSTINE

Watch, Lord, with those who wake or weep tonight.
Give the angels and saints charge over those who sleep.
Jesus Christ, tend your sick ones,
rest your weary ones, bless your dying ones,
soothe the suffering ones,
pity all the afflicted ones,
shield the joyful ones,
and all for your love's sake.
Amen.

# END OF DAY PRAYER TO GOD THE FATHER

O Eternal God and King of all creation,
who has granted me to arrive at this hour,
forgive me the sins that I have committed today in thought,
word and deed, and cleanse, O Lord, my humble soul
from all defilement of flesh and spirit.
And grant me, O Lord, to pass the sleep of this night in peace,
that when I rise from my bed I may please Your most holy
Name
and all the days of my life and conquer my flesh and the
fleshless foes that war with me
And deliver me O Lord, from vain and frivolous thoughts,
and from evil desires which defile me.
For Yours is the kingdom, the power and the glory of the
Father, Son and Holy Spirit,
now and ever, and to the ages of ages.
Amen.

*Saint Macarius the Great*

# BEDTIME PRAYER

## MATTHEW, MARK, LUKE AND JOHN - THE BLACK PATERNOSTER

Matthew, Mark, Luke and John,
Bless the bed that I lie on.
Four corners to my bed,
Four angels around my head;
One to watch and one to pray,
And two to bear my soul away.

*Traced to medieval England*

## NURSERY RHYME BEDTIME PRAYER NOW I LAY ME DOWN TO SLEEP

Now I lay me down to sleep,
I pray the Lord my soul to keep;
If I die before I wake,
I pray thee Lord my soul to take. Amen.

*Thomas Fleet*


## UPON LYING DOWN, AND GOING TO SLEEP

Here I lay me down to sleep.
To thee, O Lord, I give my Soul to keep,
Wake I ever, Or, wake I never;
To thee O Lord, I give my Soul to keep forever.

*George Wheeler*

# NIGHT PRAYER

*NOW THE DAY IS OVER*

Now the day is over,
night is drawing near;
shadows of the evening
steal across the sky.

Jesus, give the weary
calm and sweet repose;
with your tenderest blessing
may my eyelids close.

Comfort every sufferer
watching late in pain;
those who plan some evil,
from their sin restrain.

Through the long night-watches
may your angels spread
their bright wings above me,
watching round my bed.

When the morning wakens,
then may I arise
pure and fresh and sinless
in your holy eyes.

*Sabine Baring-Gould*

## GRACE BEFORE MEALS

Dear Lord, thank you for this food we are about to eat.
We are grateful for Your provision.
We ask that You would bless this food
and continue to guide our family along Your path.
In the name of Your son, Jesus.
Amen


Lord God, Heavenly Father,
bless us and these Thy gifts which we receive
from Thy bountiful goodness, through Jesus Christ, our Lord.
Amen

# SPECIAL FEAST - INVOCATION

Loving God, bless all those gathered here today
as we come together in friendship and fellowship.
Thank you for the blessings of our individual
and collective God given gifts.
Place in our hearts the desire to make a difference
to our families, to our community, to our country,
and to the many cultures and peoples worldwide.
Give us balance in times of distraction and uncertainty.
Help us move towards our goals with determination
 and always with an abundant sense of humor.
Thank you for food in a world where many know only hunger;
For our faith in a world where many know fear;
For friends in a world where many know only loneliness.
Please bless this food we are about to share, those who
prepared it, those who serve it,
and those who have worked to make today the special occasion
that it is.
For all of this we give you thanks.

*Izola White*

# GLORIA PATRI - ROMAN RITE LATIN VERSION

Glory to the Father,
and to the Son
and to the Holy Spirit,
as it was in the beginning,
Is now and ever shall be,
world without end.
Amen

# TO HIM BE THE POWER

And now to Him who is able to keep us from falling,
and lift us from the dark valley of despair
to the bright mountain of hope,
from the midnight of desperation to the daybreak of joy;
to Him be the power and authority for ever and ever.
Amen

*Martin Luther King Jr.*

# THY GLORY'S LIGHT

0 light supreme, by mortal thought unscanned...
O highest Light,
lifted up so far above all mortal thinking,
lend my mind,
a little of what you're like.
One single spark of all Thy glory's light.

*Dante Alighieri*

## ST. CHRYSOSTOM'S DAY PRAYER

O Lord, deprive me not of Your heavenly joys.
If I have sinned in mind or thought,
in word or deed, forgive me.
Deliver me from ignorance, forgetfulness, cowardice and stony
insensibility. Deliver me from temptation.
Enlighten my heart which evil desires have darkened.
Lord I being human have sinned,
but You being the generous God, have mercy on me,
knowing the sickness of my soul,
send Your grace to my help,
that I may glorify Your holy name.
Write me Your servant in the Book of Life,
and grant me a good end.
God, even though I have done nothing good in Your sight,
yet grant me by Your grace to make a good start.
Sprinkle into my heart the dew of Your grace.
Lord of heaven and earth remember me,
Your sinful servant, in Your Kingdom.
Amen.

## ST. CHRYSOSTOM'S NIGHT PRAYER

O Lord, accept me in penitence. Leave me not. Lead me not into
temptation.
Grant me good thoughts,
Lord, grant me tears and remembrance of death and compunction.
Grant me the thought of confessing my sins. Grant me humility,
chastity and obedience. Grant me patience, courage and meekness.
Plant in me the root of all blessings, the fear of
You in my heart. Grant me to love
You and always to do Your will.
Protect me from certain people and demons of passion, and from
every other harmful thing
May Your will be also in me, a sinner, for blessed are You forever.
Amen

*Saint John Chrysostom*

## ACT OF CONTRITION

Dear God, I am sorry for my sins with all my heart.
In choosing to do wrong and failing to do good,
but most of all because they offend You,
who are all good and deserving of all my love.
I firmly intend, with the help of Your grace,
to confess my sins, to do penance,
amend my life, and to avoid whatever leads me to sin.
God, have mercy.
Amen

*From the Sacrament of Penance*

# O GLADSOME LIGHT

Alleluia, Alleluia.
Joyous, holy light of the glory of the immortal, heavenly,
holy Father: Jesus Christ. Having come to the setting of the sun,
we have seen this evening light.
Let us praise the Father, the Son, and the Holy Spirit of God,
and together let us say, "Amen."
Make us worthy for all time to bless with a voice,
with a song, the name of glory of the all-holy Trinity who has
given life,
and for which the world glorifies thee.

*From the Apostolic Constitutions*

## MORNING PRAYER FROM UTILE FLOWER, A CARMELITE NUN

Dear God! I ask thee for myself and for those whom I hold dear,
the grace to fulfill perfectly Thy Holy Will,
to accept for love of Thee the joys and sorrows of this passing life,
so that we may one day be united together in Heaven for all Eternity.
Amen.

*Saint Therese of Lisieux*

# BOOKMARK OF SAINT TERESA OF AVILA

Let nothing disturb you.
Let nothing frighten you.
All things pass.
God does not change.
Patience achieves everything.
Whoever has God, lacks nothing.
God alone suffices.
Christ has no body now on earth but yours;
no hands but yours; no feet but yours.
Yours are the eyes through which the compassion of Christ,
must look out on the world.
Yours are the feet with which He is to go about doing good.
Yours are the hands with which He is to bless His people.

# PRAYER OF SAINT THOMAS AQUINAS

Grant me grace,
O merciful God,
to desire ardently all that is pleasing to You;
to examine it prudently,
to acknowledge it truthfully,
and to accomplish it perfectly.
For the praise and glory of Your name.
Amen.

## ADORO TE DEVOTE

I devoutly adore you, hidden deity.
Who are truly hidden beneath these appearances.
My whole heart submits to You,
because in contemplating You, it is fully deficient.
Sight, touch, taste, all fail in their judgement of You.
But hearing suffices firmly to believe.
I believe all that the Son of God has spoken;
there is nothing truer than this word of truth.
On the cross only the divinity was hidden,
but here the humanity is also hidden,
yet believing and confessing both,
I ask for what the penitent thief asked.
I do not see wounds as Thomas did,
but I confess that You are my God.
Make me believe much more in You,
hope in You, and love You.
0 memorial of our Lord's death,
Living Bread that gives life to man,
grant my soul to live on You,
and always to savor your sweetness.
Lord Jesus, Good Pelican,
clean me, the unclean, with Your blood,
one drop of which can heal
the entire world of all its sins.
Jesus, whom now I see hidden,
I ask You to fulfill what I so desire:
That the sight of Your Face being unveiled
I may have the happiness of seeing Your Glory.
Amen.

*Saint Thomas Aquinas*

# SAINT IGNATIUS LOYOLA'S PRAYER

Take Lord, and receive all my liberty,
my memory, my understanding,
and my entire will;
All I have and call my own.
You have given all to me.
To you, Lord, I return it.
Everything is yours; do with it what you will.
Give me only your love and your grace,
that is enough for me.

# PRAYER OF SAINT TERESA OF CALCUTTA

The fruit of Silence is Prayer.
The fruit of Prayer is Faith.
The fruit of Faith is Love.
The fruit of Love is Service.
Amen.

## PRAYER FOR FINAL PERSEVERANCE

Our dear Redeemer,
relying on your promises,
because you are faithful, all powerful and merciful,
we hope, through the merits of your passion,
for the forgiveness of our sins,
perseverance until death in your grace;
and at length we hope, by your mercy,
to see and love your eternally in heaven.
Amen.

*Saint Alphonsus Ligouri*

## JUST FOR TODAY

My life is but an instant, a passing hour.
My life is but a day that escapes and flies away.
O my God! You know that to love you on earth,
I only have today.
God, what does it matter if the future is gloomy?
To pray for tomorrow, oh no, I can not.
Keep my heart pure, cover me with your light, just for today.
0 divine pilot, whose hand guides me;
I am soon to see you on the eternal shore.
Guide my little boat over the stormy waves in peace,
just for today.
Amen.

*Saint Therese of Lisieux*

# MORNING PSALM

Let me hear Your loving kindness in the morning;
For I trust in You;
Teach me the way in which I should walk;
For to You I lift my soul.

*Psalm 143:8*

# PSALM WHEN IN FEAR

Even though I walk through the
valley of the shadow of death,
I will fear no evil, for You are always with me.

*Psalm 23:4*

# SELECTED VERSES FROM PSALMS

O Lord, you are our home,
to whom we fly,
And so has always been from age to age;
Before the hills did intercept the eye.
Before the frame was up of earthly stage.
One God you were,
and are and still shall be;
The line of time,
it does not measure You.

Both death and life obey your holy lore,
And visit in their turns, as they are sent;
A thousand years with you, they are no more than yesterday,
which is here and spent:
Or as a watch that keeps the course of time,
and comes and goes, unaware to them that sleep.

Teach us Lord, to number well our days,
Thereby our hearts to wisdom to apply;
For that which guides man best in all his ways,
Is meditation of mortality,
This bubble light, this vapor of our breath,
Teach us to consecrate to hour of material death.

God return unto us and balance now,
with days of joy, our sorrows.
Begin your work, in this our age.
The glorious majesty of God above,
shall ever reign in mercy and in love.
As long as I have being,
I will praise The works of God,
and all his wondrous ways.

# PRAYER OF THOMAS a KEMPIS

God, our Father,
we are exceedingly frail and indisposed to every virtuous and
gallant undertaking.
Strengthen our weakness, we beseech you,
that we may do valiantly in this spiritual war;
help us against our own negligence and cowardice,
and defend us from the treachery of our unfaithful hearts.
For Jesus Christ's sake.

*Thomas a Kempis*

# WE REMEMBER THEM

When we are weary and in need of strength
When we are lost and sick at heart,
We remember them.

When we have a joy we crave to share
When we have decisions that are hard to make
When we have achievements that are based on theirs,
We remember them.

At the blowing of the wind and in the chill of winter
At the opening of the buds and in the rebirth of spring
We remember them.

At the blueness of the skies and in the warmth of summer
At the rustling of the leaves and in the beauty of autumn
We remember them.

At the rising of the sun and at its setting
We remember them.

As long as we live, they too will live; for they are now part of us
As we remember them.

*Adapted from the Jewish Prayer Book*

# THOUGHTS IN SOLITUDE

My Lord God, I have no idea where I'm going,
I do not see the road ahead of me.
I can not know for certain where it will end,
nor do I really know myself.
And the fact that I think I'm following your will,
does not mean that I'm actually doing so.
But I believe that the desire to please you,
does in fact please you.
And I hope I have that desire in all that I'm doing.
And I know if I do this, you will lead me by the right road,
though I may know nothing about it.
Therefore, I will trust you always.
Though I may seem to be lost and in the shadow of death;
I will not fear, for you are ever with me.
And you will never leave me to face my perils alone.

*Thomas Merton*

# SPIRIT DIVINE, ATTEND OUR PRAYERS

Spirit divine, attend our prayers,
and make this house thy home;
descend with all thy gracious powers,
O come, great spirit, come!

Come as the light; to us reveal our emptiness and woe,
and lead us in those paths of life, whereon the righteous go.
Come as the fire and purge our hearts like sacrificial flame;
let our whole soul and offering be to our Redeemer's name.

Come as the dove, and spread thy wings,
the wings of peaceful love;
and let thy church on earth become,
blessed as the church above.

Come as the dew and sweetly bless
this consecrated hour;
may barrenness rejoice
to own thy fertilizing power.

Spirit divine, attend our prayers,
make a lost world thy home;
descend with all thy gracious powers;
O come, great spirit, come!

*Andrew Reed*

# IN TIMES OF SORROW

May you see God's light on the path ahead
When the road you walk is dark.
May you always hear,
Even in your hour of sorrow,
The gentle singing of the lark.
When times are hard, may hardness
Never turn your heart to stone,
May you always remember
when the shadows fall,
You do not walk alone.

*Author unknown*

# WE GIVE THANKS

We thank you for all the things that did not come to bother us,
For burdens we did not bear,
For troubles that passed us by,
For tasks we did not fail to do,
For hurts we did not keep;
For the friend who did not prove untrue,
For the joy that did not perish.
We give thanks for the blinding storm, that did not loose its
swelling; And for the sudden harm, that came not near our
dwelling.
We thank you for unsent munitions, And for the bitter word
unspoken,
For lives remaining, for the tears not shed,
And for the heart ties that are still unbroken.

*Author unknown*

## PEACE TO YOU

Deep peace of the running wave to you,
Deep peace of the flowing air to you,
Deep peace of the quiet earth to you,
Deep peace of the shining stars to you,
Deep peace of the Son of Peace to you, forever.

*Source unknown - early Scottish*

www.ingramcontent.com/pod-product-compliance
Lightning Source LLC
Chambersburg PA
CBHW050444150626
46551CB00028B/1469